Sir Lancelot
and the
Black Knight

Tony Mitton
Illustrated by Arthur Robins

CRAZY CAMELOT

MEET THE KNIGHTS OF THE ROUND TABLE:

King Arthur
with his sword so bright,

Sir Percival,
a wily knight.

Sir Kay,
a chap whose hopes are high,

Sir Lancelot,
makes ladies sigh.

Sir Gawain,
feeling rather green,

Sir Galahad,
so young and keen.

Sir Ack,
who's fond of eating lots,

Sir Mordred,
hatching horrid plots.

Morgana,
Arthur's wicked
sister,

Merlin.
That's me,
your wizard mister!

To Sir Fraser Launchbury
& the Lady Imogen, from Scribe Tony

To Sir Hayden Thomas Skerry,
from Arthur Robins

ORCHARD BOOKS
96 Leonard Street, London EC2A 4XD
Orchard Books Australia
32/45-51 Huntley Street, Alexandria, NSW 2015
First published in Great Britain in 2003
First paperback edition 2004
Text © Tony Mitton 2003
Illustrations © Arthur Robins 2003
The rights of Tony Mitton to be identified as the author
and Arthur Robins as the illustrator of this work
have been asserted by them in accordance with the
Copyright, Designs, and Patents Act, 1988.
A CIP catalogue record for this book is available
from the British Library.
ISBN 1 84121 720 4 (hardback)
ISBN 1 84121 722 0 (paperback)
1 3 5 7 9 10 8 6 4 2 (hardback)
1 3 5 7 9 10 8 6 4 2 (paperback)
Printed in Great Britain

In the days of Merrie England
when men wore metal suits,
they had to use a spanner
to change their clanky boots.

They had to oil their armour
to stop the rust and squeaks.
And they never changed their underwear,
except when there were leaks.

The knights of Crazy Camelot,
with Arthur as their Lord,
went seeking brave adventures
to stop them getting bored.

I am the wizard Merlin.
I have a magic mind.
It's full of knightly stories.
Let's see what I can find.

I'll peer into my crystal ball,
my wizard's telly set.
I'll wave my hands across it
to see what I can get.

Aha! Now this is Lancelot,
who loves a daring quest.
Of this tough chap there's many a rap,
but here's the very best.

It all began when young King Arthur
opened up his map,
and, pointing with his finger,
he gave an anxious tap.

"I hear bad news of Astolat,
from folk who've travelled there.
They say it's like a wasteland now,
all drab and bleak and bare.

"So who will go and scout about
to see what they can see?"
Sir Lancelot was quick to cry,

I will, Sire.
Please... Send me!

So Arthur sent Sir Lancelot,
his Champion Number One,
a wondrous sight in armour bright
that sparkled in the sun.

But when he got to Astolat
the sun began to fade.
And soon he found that all around
there hung a gloomy shade.

The crops were withered on their stalks.
The grass was dry and brown.
And few folk seemed to be about,
even in the town.

If Lancelot saw people,
he'd wave to them and call.
But as he rode to meet them,
they'd scarper, one and all!

So Lancelot tried knocking,
but no one dared to answer.
Not even to Sir Lancelot,
the King's most famous lancer!

Now night was falling, so he searched
for somewhere he could sleep.
He found a tumbled haystack
and soon lay snoring deep.

But in the dark Sir Lancelot
sat up with beating heart.
A sense of someone watching him
had given him a start.

It was a maid so pale and fair
with wide and watery eyes.
When Lancelot caught sight of her,
he sprang up in surprise!

"What's going on? Now who are you?
What are you doing here?"
cried Lancelot. And yet the maid
just looked at him in fear.

"Now answer me at once!" he snapped,
"Or I'll go nuts and yell."
The poor maid started weeping
and then began to tell.

"My father was Lord Astolat,
but now, alas, he's dead.
A horrid knight, all clad in black,
is ruling us instead.

"He keeps our country captive.
He holds us in his spell.
He says that he will squidge us,
if we should dare to tell."

"I'll dent his horrid helmet,"
Sir Lancelot cried out.
"The very thought of such a villain
makes me want to shout."

I'll take my trusty broadsword
and give his bonce a bang.
I'll cut his coward's shield in half
and make his breastplate clang.

"If you would fight this nasty knight,"
the maid said, "come with me.
The spooky old Sad Chapel
is where he soon will be."

She led Sir Lancelot away
and through a scary wood,
until they reached a clearing
where a ruined chapel stood.

Around the walls were hung the shields
of many a valiant knight.
They'd come to sort this villain out,
but gone and lost the fight.

"To meet this knight," the maid explained,
"you must wait here till dawn.
At sun's first ray he comes this way.
You'll hear him blow his horn.

"I must go home before he comes.
My castle's on the plain.
Drop by for breakfast if you win.
Oh, yes - I'm called Elaine."

And I am bold Sir Lancelot.
I'll call by when I've won.
A spot of brekky would be nice.
I like my eggs well done.

And so he settled down to wait,
preparing for the fight,
until, at dawn, a blast of horn
brought on the big Black Knight.

His horse was black, his shield was black,
as also was his armour.
His nails were black, his teeth were black.
He truly was no charmer.

"Aha!" he growled. "O-ho!" he howled.

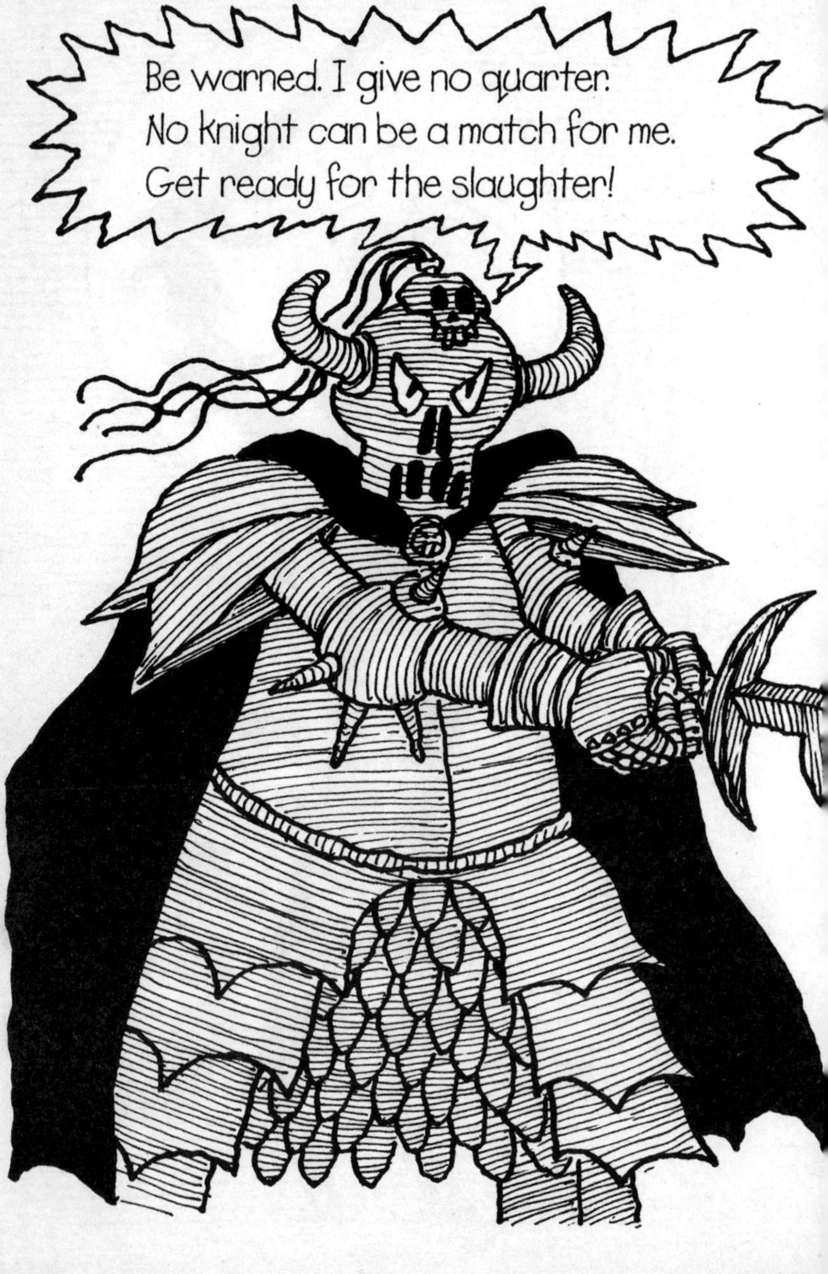

"Oh, really?" scoffed our hero.

Then give me your best shot.
But let me say that, come what may,
you won't beat Lancelot!

They hacked about. They thwacked
  about.
They biffed and bonged and banged.
They whacked about. They clacked
  about.
They clanked and clonked and clanged.

The Black Knight was enormous.
He'd make a bull feel queasy.
"To win will not," thought Lancelot,
"be quite so quick and easy..."

But Lancelot was nimble,
and Lancelot was smart.
At home he'd strained and truly trained
to master martial art.

Each time the Black Knight's
    deadly strokes
came whizzing through the air,
Sir Lancelot would dodge and duck
and hardly turn a hair.

But every blow our hero gave,
however meanly meant,
just bounced right off the
  Black Knight's armour,
leaving not a dent.

The metal had some magic
a sword could not get through.
When fighting spells and spooky stuff,
what is a knight to do?

So Lancelot looked carefully
to find a tiny chink.
"Aha!" he cried. "Just there I've spied,
yes, could it be? I think...

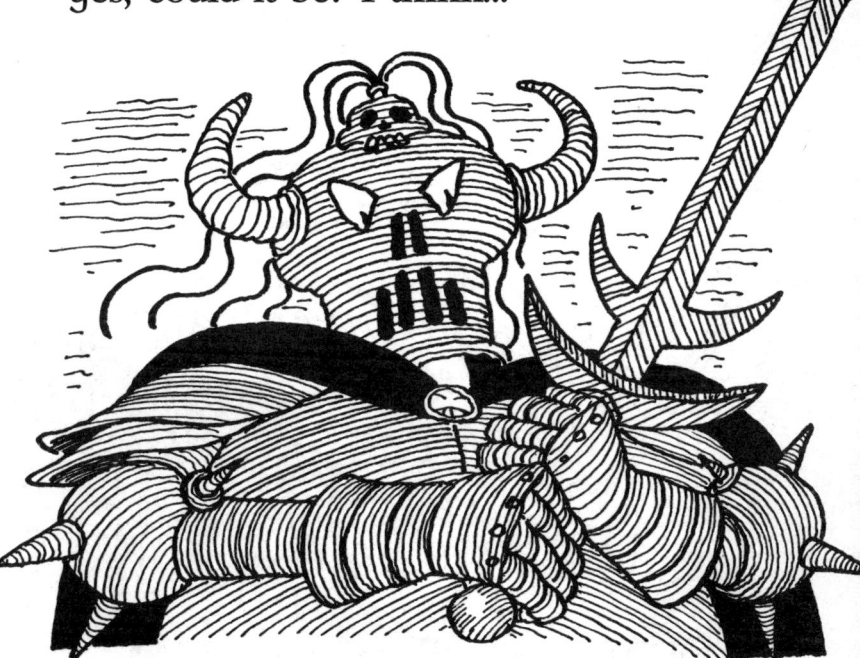

"Is that a narrow gap I see,
around the Black Knight's neck?
I'll strike him on that very spot,
or do my best, by heck!"

He ducked and dodged and
    aimed his blade.
It hit the knight right there...
And, blow me down!
    The Black Knight's head
went whirling through the air!

It landed very neatly
in the branches of a tree.
And then the head quite crossly said,

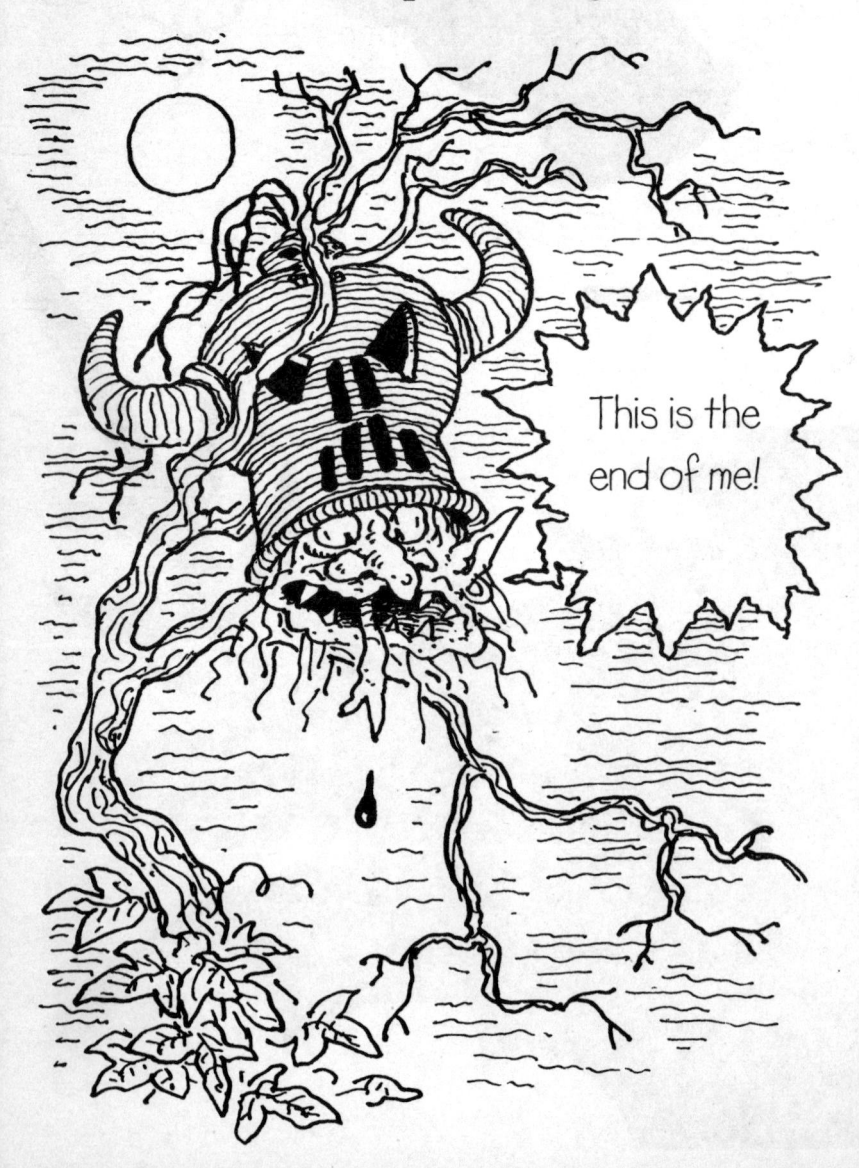

This is the end of me!

"A ghost knight," breathed Sir Lancelot.
"A phantom! By my beard!"
And as he spoke, the strange spell broke.
The Black Knight disappeared.

The horse, the head, the armour,
left not a single trace.
"It's time to go," thought Lancelot.
"What a creepy place!"

He swiftly left that spooky wood
and rode across the plain.
The Land of Astolat shone bright
and happy once again.

And folk came dancing out of doors
with cries of joy and glee,

So Lancelot got breakfast,
as promised by the maid.
She cooked a pan of scrambled eggs
with toast and marmalade.

The eggs were hot and tasty.
The toast was fresh and thin.
But the marmalade was best of all,
for that had magic in.

"This marmalade's delicious,"
Sir Lancelot declared.
And as he munched he gazed at her,
and stared and stared and stared.

Elaine had put a potion in
to liven up his snack.
You see, she'd got a crush on him,
and now, he'd love her back.

She couldn't bear to see him leave,
this brave and hunky Sir.
That's why she spiked the marmalade -
to make him fancy her.

So let's leave brave Sir Lancelot
and beautiful Elaine
to spend some time together
on Astolat's fair plain.

The bad Black Knight is conquered.
The daring quest has ended.
And, for the folk of Astolat,
things are mostly mended.

Now, here's a little exit trick
for you to marvel at.
I stretch my arms, say magic charms
and WHAMMO! I'm a bat.

CRAZY CAMELOT CAPERS

Written by Tony Mitton
Illustrated by Arthur Robins

Crazy Camelot Capers are available from all good bookshops,
or can be ordered direct from the publisher:
Orchard Books, PO BOX 29, Douglas IM99 1BQ
Credit card orders please telephone 01624 836000
or fax 01624 837033
or e-mail: bookshop@enterprise.net for details.

To order please quote title, author and ISBN
and your full name and address.
Cheques and postal orders should be
made payable to 'Bookpost plc'.
Postage and packing is FREE within the UK
(overseas customers should add £1.00 per book).

Prices and availability are subject to change.